CW00747267

Huntington Revisited

Colin Carr

© Colin Carr 2009

Published by Carbeck Publications

Revised Edition 2012

ISBN 978 0 9561876 0 4

All rights reserved. Reproduction of this book by photocopying or electronic means for non-commercial purposes is permitted. Otherwise, no part of this book may be reproduced, adapted, stored in a retrieval system or transmitted by any means, electronic, mechanical, photocopying, or otherwise without the prior written permission of the author.

Cover picture by Charles Bowerman: Mr Walter Yates and daughter Kath

Prepared and printed by:
York Publishing Services
64 Hallfield Road
Layerthorpe
York YO31 7ZQ
Tel: 01904 431213
www.yps-publishing.co.uk

Acknowledgements

Some of the photographs contained in this book, have been taken by the well known Huntington photographer and artist Mr. Charles Bowerman, who captured the ambience of the original Huntington village on film. He and others, who very kindly donated photographs, are credited as they appear, and to whom I offer my sincerest thanks. Those that are not credited are either my own, or by persons unknown, who despite my best efforts was unable to locate for inclusion in this acknowledgement.

I must also show my appreciation to all those good people of Huntington who have helped me complete this project by offering their local memories of a bygone age, in particular the Huntington Parish Council for their encouragement and commitment to purchase many copies to distribute within the local community. My sincere thanks also go to my wife Carol for her patience, understanding and putting up with me hogging her computer. I am also indebted to Carol for using her artistic skills in painting the 'barge passing under Dowker's bridge' picture on page 34, John Lacy for allowing me to use photos from his family collection and also to Barry Beckwith for his help with computer compilation and graphics work. Barry worked for many years, prior to retirement, providing IT and desktop publishing services for the City of York council. Without his help, and the many hours he has worked putting his skill to good use, my book may not have come to fruition.

My thanks go to the following for permission to reproduce extracts from their publications: Joyce Petch – *The Centenary of Huntington Methodist Church*, Fred Robinson – *A History of Huntington Church*, Mike Fife and Peter Walls – *The River Foss*.

Back Lane in the winter of 1940

Photo: Charles Bowerman

The Old Village

Photo: J.C. Lacy

The cottages featured were situated on the corner of what is currently opposite of the Huntington Road end of New Lane. They were owned by the township, and were let to an interesting series of tenants, two of whom were William Bowl and Francis Lonsdale. Records show that in April 1843 they were given a month's notice to pay rent arrears. Vestry meeting records stated in 1845 that it was: 'resolved that an act of the very immoral conduct of some of the inmates of the houses occupied by F.Lonsdale, Geo. Toes and Jnr. Carter and that without considerable amendment of such conduct the Overseers of Poor proceed in the regular way to dispossess them.' It is left to the reader's imagination as to the details of this eviction. John Dennison was paid £1:0s:06d for sixty one and a half straw bricks, and Ben Wood was paid 12s:03d for thatching in 1847. In 1800 Huntington already had several houses which were over 100 years old. Most of the houses in the village were brick and tiled with only a few thatched roofs. Agriculture was the main activity in the Huntington area, and in 1850, over a distance of a mile; there were 25 farms with an average size being 35 acres worked by 15 farmers. The 1801 census shows Huntington to have a population of 312. By 1851 it had risen to 416.

Photo: J.C. Lacy

The Lodge

A senior director of Rowntrees (now Nestlé) Albert Norton, once lived here, and had a wrought iron gate made with his and his wife's initials included in the design. The Lodge was also known as 'The Hutt'.

Photo: Don Copley

Fire Insurance Plaque

An interesting feature of this building is that it has a fire insurance plaque on the wall. Many years ago, Insurance companies had their own firemen, which were probably two men with a horse and cart with a large tub of water and several buckets. Well off people could afford to insure their property against fire, and in the event of a fire, the firemen would only tend the fire at the house with the plaque, if the fire spread to the house next door, it was the problem of the occupants. By the time the Insurance Company had been informed, and the firemen had saddled the horses up, then driven to the site of the fire, the house would probably have burned down.

Clematis

This house was renovated in the 1980's and as the name suggests, Clematis plants would have grown there. Clematis still grows nearby in the grounds of the former stables of the lodge which has been converted to a house.

Photo: Joyce Turner

The Hazels

The Hazels, was situated at the Huntington Road end of the Old Village. The Magson family took up residence in 1931, and Neville (Nev) Magson, a child at the time, remembers being fascinated by the electric lights, and he ran from one room to another switching them on and off. The house adjoined Hazel cottage. The Hazel's was purchased in 1966 by the Huntington Working Men's Club. The club had earlier built a new concert room, but the architects failed to realize during the planning stage, that the delivery vehicles were unable to pass between the end of the new room and the Hazels. Thus the fate of the old building was sealed and it was demolished.

Photo: J. C. Lacy

View looking down the village from the Huntington Road end towards what was formerly the White Horse Inn.

The Reading Room

As a result of funding via public subscription, the Reading Room was built in 1884. It afforded the community the opportunity to read newspapers, periodicals and any of the one hundred books on the shelves. Nathan Bellerby who was at the time Headmaster of the Board School, was appointed as Secretary in 1890, and was later succeeded by Mr. R. J. Wolstenholm.

The picture on the left, now a house and situated on the right hand side, about seventy yards from Huntington WMC, was formerly a shop used by a gent's outfitters and at one time Lund's the Grocers. (*See right*)

Imeson's Farm

This house was originally Imeson's farmhouse, which was next door to the Lund's shop. Cattle were kept next to the house during the winter. To the rear was an orchard which stretched as far as the Back Lane.

Trent Cottage

The Pearson family who lived here for many years, kept pigs and other livestock on land to the rear. This house which was situated on the right hand side, further along from Imeson's farm, was formerly two separate cottages, and was converted during the 1930s into one house. Thelma Pearson aged five, standing at the door.

Photo: J. C. Lacy

The New Willows

Formerly 'Grey Willows', this house which stood on the left hand side about fifty yards from Church Lane, was very distinctive because of the two turret corners on each side, complete with a 'spike' on each rooftop. The Shaw family lived here, and often held garden parties in the grounds to raise money for the Memorial Hall.

Glenholm

The Leeming family lived here for many years. Mrs Leeming was a very staunch member of the Womens Institute, during the war, she organised the billeting of 300 evacuees from a School in Hull. Eventually, her daughter Nancy moved in with her family, the Brayshaws.

Mr Leeming was a keen gardener, and roses covered much of the wall at the rear of the house, the garden went as far as the river Foss.

The Leeming couple were very popular with their family, when Mr Leeming died, his Grandson, David, still in his teens, wrote a very moving tribute to him.

My Grandads House by David Brayshaw

My Grandads house is ours now, we used to come round from our house, to watch T.V. because we didn't have one. I can't remember what we used to watch, maybe the adverts. There was a climbing rose on the back wall, and a long lawn with a greenhouse and pigsty. My Grandad was always in the greenhouse with his marrows. The garden went down to the river Foss. My brother and I used to hang action men on the trees and fire arrows at them, and we used to come here for Bonfire Night. My Grandads garden had a small pond, with frogs, and there were sheets of corrugated iron near the hens and the gooseberries, which always had mice under them, and there was always hedgehogs there. There was a chestnut tree in the field opposite, where houses are now, and we picked up the fallen conkers. My Grandads house had everything, "Grandad, have you got a ___?" "I'll look in my shed!" "Have you got a rocket to go to the moon?" "I'll look in my shed, I"m sure I saw one last week, if not I'll make one." My Grandads shed had everything, tins, boxes, tubs, tools, chests everything labled just in case, the shed had a smell of its own. His house smelt fusty and old, and of Woodbines, it was always dark, and smelt of new bread. I remember the fat black woman on the wall in porcelain, in her apron, with a smile and a notebook and pencil I remember the clock that isn't there anymore, the cool pantry, the red tiled floor, and I thought it had ghosts and secret passage ways.

My Grandad had kind eyes, with smile lines in the corners, I expect you could say he was tougher than the rest of the family, he used to get told off for swearing from my Grandma, when all he used to say was "WHIST!", he had silver hair and a moustache. Grandma seemed to worship him. My Grandad died in hospital, but he came home before he went to say goodbye, and I cried. I would have cried when my Grandma died too, she suffered the most. Grandad was a Sergeant in the Army, and I can remember his photograph well.

Sergeant Leeming in uniform during the First World War

My Grandads house is ours now he's gone, it doesn't look like his house now, but when I go into the front hall, near the front door, I can see them both, the smells of the old house are in that hall, and their ghosts are with us, i can smell them, and I can see things how they used to be and their spirits will always be with me.

Photo: J. C. Lacy

Clock Cottage

According to a map of Huntington in 1893, the left-hand cottage was the Post Office. The sub-postmaster was a tailor called Thomas Pick. He used to sit cross-legged on a table at the window sewing. Huntington church records show that in 1882, the public subscribed to a clock, which was to be placed on the wall of the building at a cost of £8.10s which was very expensive in those days. In the 1950's, Mr. George Magson, a local builder who was doing alterations there, discovered an ancient inglenook fireplace, estimated as being 350 years old. His father lived there around 1875. The owner at the time of the alterations was Dr. N. C. Porter, who decided he would like the fireplace restored to its original state. Iron grating, and an overhead canopy was made by village blacksmith George Wain.

Photo: J. C. Lacy

Church Lane

Very little has changed down Church Lane in the last one hundred years. The old gas lamp on the left has long gone. The house on the right was badly damaged during the Second World War, when an aircraft crashed on it, and was rebuilt after the war (*see page 28*).

Photo: J. C. Lacy

Church Lane looking towards the Old Village. These two boys are probably taking the carthorse to Church Farm in the early 1900s.

Prospect House

Photo: Mr and Mrs D Chivers

The Watson family lived in this house which is opposite Church Lane, for many years. Maurice Watson senior, an agricultural engineer, operated a threshing machine pulled by a traction engine, which he took to local farms at harvest time. His son, Maurice junior, had two coaches which he kept on Imeson's land, and took parties of day trippers to the coast. One of his specialities was organising trips to the well known open air theatre at Scarborough in the 1950s and 1960s. When I was with Huntington scout band, he often took us to band contests. There was also a younger son called Peter that I knew from school. Tragically, he was killed in a car crash soon after he was married, in his early twenties.

Below is an aerial view showing the rear of Prospect House on the right, in the 1950s when it was a farm. It shows the farmyard, cows grazing in a field and an allotment. All this farming area has since had residential properties built on it.

Photo: Mr and Mrs D Chivers

The Old Post Office

Mrs. M. Magson, the Postmistress, had two daughters and two sons. The girls worked in the Post Office which was on the left hand side about one hundred yards past Church Lane, and the boys were carters and worked on contract for Rowntrees. It is claimed you could set your watch each morning and evening as they passed going to and returning from work.

Galtres House

Situated opposite the Post Office, this was the vicar's residence before construction of the vicarage in 1902. The Macauley family lived here in the 1940s.

The Old Village Smithy

The original smith's forge was next to the Blacksmiths Arms, until it moved over the road to the rear of a house called The Walnuts in the year 1900. In 1867, there were two blacksmiths, Wm. Appleyard and John Harland. Tom Wain came later, and his son George who followed him was to be the last village blacksmith.

The Walnuts

The Walnuts, so called because there was a walnut tree in the front garden, was demolished in 2008 and a new house was built. The area to the rear has been landscaped, and a brick cycle shed has been built on the original site of the old forge.

Mille Crux Terrace

Photo: J. C. Lacy

The name Mille Crux is Latin for 'a thousand crosses'. It is my theory that the five terraced houses have been so named because of the close proximity to the Butter Cross at the end of Church Lane.

Two old houses restored and looking as good as new which are almost opposite Mille Crux.

Jonah's Shop

Jonah Nielson took over the shop from his father. He was very well known for his friendly personality and his distinctive eye patch, which made him look very dashing. It was a general store which sold almost everything. If he hadn't got what you wanted, the next time he went to town, he would get it for you. The original shop was built of wood, but in 1958, Tony Roberts built a brick one on the outside of the original shop, it never closed whilst it was being built.

The village bakery (*above*) was owned and run by Wademan's until a few years ago. The building is still known as The Bakery.

Bullock's Farm and Shop

The outbuildings

The Hare and Hounds pub eventually became a farmhouse and shop. John Bullock ran the farm which became known as White Horse Farm and his wife ran the shop. The outbuildings went right back to a large house called The White House which faced the garage. Early in the 1900s, a carter called Ambrose Todd operated from the farm. In the 1960s it became a riding school.

The White House

In the 1960s, the farm out buildings became the stable area for the White Horse Riding School, which later moved to North Moor Lane.

Bullock's Shop Corner

Photo: J. C. Lacy

View from Bullock's Corner down Strensall Road in the direction of Strensall.

Bullock's Corner is located where the Old Village meets the North Moor and Strensall Roads. Bullock's grocery shop overlooked this junction. It is no longer a shop, and is a private house known as 'The Coach House'.

Photo: J. C. Lacy

View from Strensall Road from the direction of Strensall towards Bullock's Corner.

Photo: J. C. Lacy

Colonel Palmer was very well known in the village and lived in the house on the left. He was a very keen horseman. Stables and a paddock were at the rear. This house is on the left about fifty yards from Bullock's Corner.

The well known milk lady, Miss Hare, lived for many years in the house on the right, which is opposite Bullock's Corner.

Field View

Ambrose Todd

Early in the 1900s, Ambrose Todd was a carter, and kept his horse and cart in the out buildings behind Bullocks Farm. He lived at an old house called 'Field View', which was knocked down in circa 1960s, and a bungalow was built behind the site of the house. The bill shown below from 1937, illustrates that as well as being a carter, he was a coal and coke merchant. his sons were successful in building their own business, Reg and Eric built houses in Broom close and Linden Close.

DELIVERY NOTE	Date Delivered *Nov 30* 193

AMBROSE TODD,
Coal and Coke Merchant :: Carting Contractor
Agricultural and General Work
Orders promptly delivered — Large or small

FIELD VIEW, HUNTINGTON,
TELEPHONE YORK 8224. **1188**

Mr *The Sec Committee of Management*
Memorial Hall Huntington

Take notice that you are to receive herewith the undermentioned coal in — 1 cwt. bags

	Tons	Cwts.	Lbs.	Quality	Rate	£	s.	d.
Gross weight of Coal and Vehicle &c	2		0	*Large gas*	Per Ton			
Tare weight of Vehicle	2	0	0	*coke*				
Nett weight of Coal herewith delivered to purchaser					Total		9	2

Received £9/2 with Thanks 9/1,
Delivered by *T*
Waggon No.

Where Coal is delivered by means of a vehicle, the seller must deliver or send by post or otherwise to the purchaser or his servant, before any part of the Coal is unloaded, a ticket or note in this form.
Any seller of Coal who delivers a less quantity than is stated in this ticket or note is liable to a fine.
Any person attending on a vehicle used for the delivery of Coal who having received a ticket or note for delivery to the purchaser, refuses or neglects to deliver it to the purchaser or his servant is liable to a fine.
Any error or complaint about above consignment or carter, must be reported to us within 48 hours following delivery.

Rosedene

In the 1800s, a doctor who lived here converted the house to accommodate patients with metal illnesses, the walls were padded and the yard at the rear of the house had high walls built round it.

The Coach House

Many years ago, the 'well off' people had their own transport in the form of coaches, carriages and gigs, and were kept in a large outbuilding behind their house, known as a 'Coach House'. which protected them from the outside elements, nowadays, we put our cars in 'the garage' for the same reason. Shown here is an original coach house converted into living accommodation. I was told it was advertised for sale as 'The Old Tramshed'.

Huntington Board School

Huntington had a mixed parish school in the early 1800s. Robert Burton was in charge from 1810 to 1851. The Board School opened in 1877, and was an extension to one classroom which had been the parish school. Originally there were 45 pupils. The first headmaster was Nathan Bellerby, who also was secretary for the Reading Room. Parents had to pay for their children's education until it became free in 1891.

In 1899, Mr. Wolstenholme became headmaster, and school leaving age was increased to twelve. Mr. Sowter followed in 1932. Due to the expanding population, the school became over-crowded, and classes had to be held in the nearby Memorial Hall. Tom Appleby became headmaster in 1938, but in 1941 he transferred along with pupils over the age of eleven to the new Joseph Rowntree's Secondary Modern School in New Earswick.

The school is now the village community centre run by Mrs Maureen Duncanson.

The Schoolmaster's house is on the left.

Photo: J. C. Lacy

The class of 1914

Photo: J. C. Lacy

The population of Huntington in 1901 was 631, and by 1961 it had risen to 5,680. It was therefore necessary for the local authority to build a larger junior school which would accommodate 260 children, with a kitchen to provide school meals. From 1942 until the opening of the new school, meals were delivered by the Strensall central kitchen. The new school was officially opened in 1962 by Mrs. I.G. Wightman, B.A. J.P. the Lord Mayor of York. Two classes were held in the old school which was to be known as The Annexe. The Yearsley Grove Junior School was to follow soon after and opened in 1965. In June 1977, Mr.P.R.Webster, P.T.A. chairman, presented the school with a shield for improved work.

Photo: Pete Freeman

Mrs. E.J. Hunter, a former caretaker of the annexe for 20 years, switched on the centenary clock on July 11th 1977 *(see photo above)*. Mr. P. R. Webster PTA chairman is standing at the rear.

The Memorial Hall

The Memorial Hall was built in 1921 by the local men who returned from the First World War, and gave their services free. There is a faded plaque on the wall in the entrance listing the local men who were killed, wounded or taken prisoner. A conscientious member of staff has done a copy of the original, and has started a record of each individual soldier who died in action.

In the 1920s, the money raised at the annual Huntington Carnival provided a donation to the hall, and a grand dance was held there at the end of the carnival day. A small dance band called The BI-JU Band played there for dances, and two men from New Earswick, Reg Cooper (violin) and Stan Shuttleworth (piano) also formed the basis for another small band. The Middleton Hunt held their Hunt Balls there on many occasions, and the Women's Institute had an amateur dramatic group which put on shows. Thelma Wadsworth remembers the children from the Board School were presented with a silver spoon by Rowntree's and Co. to commemorate the coronation of King George the VI in 1937. She still has the spoon and has never had to clean it. The Hall was often used as an overflow for classes when the Board School ran out of space. In the late 1950s, a committee was formed by Mr. E. Cambridge to create a youth club, which was to be called The Silver Moor Youth Club. The club met in the hall each week, and held a dance each month. The hall is still used for a variety of events, including the pre-school playgroup and as a practice hall for York City Pipe Band.

Photo: Mrs Thelma Wadsworth

Roll of Honour

1914 - 1918

J. C. METCALF
C. E. ROBINSON
F.DUSTON
J. CUSSINS
F.P.L. MATHEWS
A. WAIND
H. ABBOTT
O. BROOKS
D. CONROY
J.G. DOUGLASS
W. MARSHALL
W. MARKS
H. TUTILL
B. SPENCER
S. WARD
P.T. HALL
J. NELSON
A.MERCER
W. BLACKURN
J. FENWICK
G. GOULDEN
H. POWELL
A.ROOKE
A. SCAIFE
J. SHAW
W. WALLS
J. WALLS
S. COLLINSON
P. SCOTT. RNAS
D.S. PATTIE

1939 - 1945

J. W. ATKINSON
E. W. BROADLEY
R. BROADLEY
C. MOUNTAIN
A. ROBINSON
R. SANDERSON
W. A. GREENWOOD
W.E. WRIGGLESWORTH
N. BECK
G. J. ELLIS
A.T. COX
A. LONG
M. R. MOXON
L. RACE
A. BONNAS
J. HUDSON
F. R. MAGSON
J. DANIELS
C. H. DANIELS
J. F. CRAIG
G. C. KIRTON
R. EASTON
A. CLOUD
J. S. HULME
E. FLOOD
K. SWAIN

Huntington in WWII

The Home Guard

Photo: Mr Philip Roe

The local home guard was made up of men from Huntington and New Earswick. The H.Q. was the coach house and stables of West Huntington Hall *(see page 35)*. They were formed into a company, and wore the cap badge of the Green Howards. Its Commanding Officer was Colonel Palmer, a former officer in the Royal Engineers. He rode on horseback on exercises, and carried a rifle in a leather case attached to the saddle. They seem to have done most of their training locally, and received an annual treat of a rabbit pie supper served up at the Huntington Working Men's Club. I would think there were plenty of rabbits in the area, as it was at the time only a small village.

My father was in this unit, and I remember him telling me that on one training exercise, his platoon were told to go to Earswick railway station and wait for the 'enemy' which were supposed to arrive by train. When it got to 1 p.m., and the "enemy" still hadn't arrived, they all went home for their dinner.

Some time during the war, the unit had a photo shoot in front of the cricket pavilion, which was on the sports field in front of Joseph Rowntree's school. The copy of the photo above was given to me by Philip Roe, whose father was also in this unit.

Eric Carr, my father in Home Guard uniform showing me the correct way to throw a Mills grenade.

In the mid-fifties, when I was very young, I lived in New Earswick. During the school holidays a friend and I went across the fields to the Westfield beck. We gathered some dry wood and lit a fire at the side of the beck. After a while we noticed some bottles containing an orange liquid, and my friend opened one. Some of the contents spilled on to his jeans, and when he went near the fire they set alight. He panicked and ran around, but he had the good sense to lie on the ground and smother the flames until they were extinguished. When he got home his mother phoned the police, who got in touch with the Army. The next day a bomb disposal unit arrived. The bottles turned out to be a cache of phosphorus bombs which had been buried by the Home Guard during the war.

Mrs. G Mills took three evacuees (three sisters from Hull) into her home during the Second World War and received the certificate above after the war for her hospitality.

More than three hundred evacuees arrived in Huntington from St. Mary's Roman Catholic School in Hull during 1939. Mrs. A Leeming, who was the local billeting officer, found temporary homes with local families that had spare rooms.

Pictured *(right)* Mrs. Holton, of Huntington, reading to six of her evacuee children – Bridget and David Harrison, of Hull, Vera and Ann Morgan, of Middlesborough, Harry Smith and Kenneth Stockhill, also of Middlesborough.

Huntington in Wartime

Rescue Services ARP and AFS

Huntington was preparing for war during 1939. Air Raid Precautions, (ARP), Auxiliary Fire Service (AFS) and Home Guard units were formed. The ARP occupied Ivy Cottage, next to the Working Men's Club, and initially the AFS kept their equipment in stables next to The Lodge. The Memorial Hall was to be the billeting centre for evacuees. Mrs. Leeming arranged for them to be billeted at local houses with spare rooms.

The ARP wardens were responsible for enforcing blackouts. If there was a chink of light showing through anyone's curtains, the warden would have to tell them very forcefully to correct it. It was an offence to have any light showing and on one occasion the Memorial Hall was fined £3 for a blackout offence. They had a switchboard so the main H.Q. in York could maintain contact with them. Air Raid Warden Ethel Morley came knocking on Thelma Pearson's door to tell them that there was a big air raid on York. The Pearson family were worried because their father worked at York Station, which was badly bombed. He returned safely in the morning after helping with rescue work.

The AFS had two trailer pumps, and which were housed with other fire fighting equipment, in two wooden huts which were built opposite the Working Men's Club on the grass verge near the vicarage. The Senior Fire officer, Sam Mills had a Ford car which was used to travel to other local units and inspect their equipment, and to also tow a fire pump. Mr. Neville (Nev) Magson remembers other firemen as being, Albert Ware, Knobby Clarke, George Rank, Maurice Watson and Tommy Jefferson. They were probably in attendance when a Wellington bomber crashed on the village *(see page 28)*. A local woman told me she was born in the fire station.

A typical wartime AFS team with a Ford V8 saloon, adapted to tow a fire pump trailer and carry a rescue ladder. The edges of the mudguards are painted white so they could be seen in the blackout.

Phoenix

The quiet life around Huntington was shattered on 14 April, 1943, when at 16.10 hrs, a MK.10 Wellington bomber from 429 Squadron, Royal Canadian Air Force, stationed at Eastmoor airfield, near Sutton on the Forest, crashed on houses opposite the Blacksmiths Arms in the Old Village. Whilst on a test flight from RAF Leeming, one of the engines caught fire, causing the

Vickers Wellington

aircraft to spin out of control over the village. The pilot, Flying Officer H.W.Gray, and four other members of the crew perished. Three elderly ladies who lived in the houses were also killed. Burning fuel turned the buildings into a raging inferno, causing severe damage. When the houses were rebuilt after the war, one was aptly named PHOENIX, and remains so to this day.

David Batters lived in one of the houses during the war, and had a very lucky escape. He was five years old at the time, and his mother had taken him to the clinic in New Earswick. On the way back, they had just passed Joseph Rowntree's School, when they noticed thick black smoke rising from the direction of Huntington. Some of their neighbours intercepted them on their return to Huntington, informed them what had happened and advised them to turn back. They returned to New Earswick and stayed with relatives. Returning to their home a few days later, they discovered that all their windows had been blown out.

D DAY – June 6 1944

I was told by Tony Roberts who lived in the old village that late in the war, large convoys of army vehicles from Strensall barracks were passing their house all night. The next day it was announced on the radio that the invasion of Normandy (D DAY) had taken place. They would have been 'follow up' troops that would reinforce the initial invasion once they had managed to get a foothold on the Normandy beaches. He remembers each vehicle 'changing down the gears' as they approached the sharp bend at Mille Crux Terrace.

The Corn Mill

At the highest point in Huntington known at the time as Hoggard's Hill, stood the corn mill. Corn had been ground there since the 13th century. No evidence has been found as to when it was built. I would guess around 1750. It ceased to be used around 1900. Records show that John Croft was the corn miller in 1823 and Charles Etty in 1890.

Mr. Derek Atlay remembers that in the 1950s the mill's circular base still remained, but had been reduced to the height of about four feet. A house was later built on the site.

Today, the base remains at ground level, and now forms the perimeter of a flower bed.

The Miller - Charles Matthew Etty

(Relation of William Etty – Painter)

The miller, Charles Mathew Etty, a relative of the well known York painter, William Etty, lived in the Mill House. Many years later it became Mill Hill shop. The mill was left derelict for many years after it stopped working, which is likely to have happened on or about the death of Charles Etty in 1897. Mr. F. Sturdy, who lived in the Mill House, thinking the mill was a danger to children demolished it, and used the bricks to build a cottage as an extension to his house, which was occupied by his mother-in-law. Miss E. M. Lacey, who lived at the Mill House in later years, when it was a shop, on enquiring as to where the windmill had gone that was at the bottom of her garden, was surprised when one of Mr. Sturdy's daughters contacted her and said the bricks from the mill had been used to build the cottage on the end of her house.

The Millers house before the extension was added

At the bottom of Mill Hill (formerly Hoggard's Hill) was a wooden bridge which formed part of the drive to West Huntington Hall. The colour painting above, shows a little brick bridge on the right. I remember this bridge in the 1950s. It always had water beneath it containing newts, minnows and red throats. It was a popular picnic spot for New Earswick people. On sunny afternoons, my mother took me there several times. When I visited this location some years ago, I was disappointed to find it had been covered over to form the flood bank. The bricks are still to be seen on the towpath. When the River Foss opened to barge traffic in about 1800, a swing bridge was built to allow access for barges. It was called Dowker's Bridge, after Captain Sir Thomas Dowker of West Huntington Hall.

Dowker's Swing Bridge

The Brick Bridge

Photo: Ian Cottom

I remember this bridge in the 1950s, it always had water beneath it containing newts, minnows and red throats, it was a popular spot for New Earswick people, my Mother took me there in Summer several times. When I visited this location some years ago, I was disappointed to find it had been covered over to form the flood bank. The bricks at the top of the bridge are still to be seen on the towpath.

Photo: River Foss Society

The Stepping Stones

Photo: River Foss Society

A young local lad treads cautiously as he makes his way across the river.

The weir on the River Foss at the New Earswick lock house close to the Link Road, was removed by German prisoners of war in 1917, lowering the water level. The first stepping stones were placed there at the time. In 1924, the parish council placed the first official stepping stones there. People of New Earswick used them as a short cut to get to the newly established Huntington W.M.C. It must have been tricky returning home after they'd had a few pints! Italian prisoners of war were employed in 1943 to clear the Foss of weeds and they replaced the original stones with some they had made. In the 1950s, I remember the fun we had as young boys playing on the stones, jumping from one to another, and one of us would always fall in. The Foss Internal Drainage Board, when clearing the river in 1971-2 removed the stones. This created friction between the parish councils of Huntington, New Earswick and the Foss Internal Drainage Board. Both Parish Councils wanted the stones replaced; claiming it was a right of way. The Drainage Board claimed they were an obstruction to the river flow. Sadly, they were not replaced, and so another part of our heritage has gone for ever. The stones are now at rest in a nearby garden.

Photo: River Foss Society

Two local men cross the river, one appears to be coaxing the dog to jump on the next stone.

Barge passing through Dowker's swing bridge – painting by Carol Carr

The Foss Navigation Company

In 1793, the company had the power to purchase lands, tenements and hereditent, and 'power to make and maintain a navigational communication for boats, barges and other vessels, from the junction of the River Foss with the river River Ouse, to Stillington Mill, which was twelve and a half miles long.' Castle Mills lock was completed in 1794, and was open to Monk Bridge by December. In 1795 work was carried out to build locks, lock keepers cottages and bridges as far as Strensall. Mr. Scruton supervised the construction of a reservoir near Yearsley, and two locks and a bridge at Strensall in 1796-7.

The whole navigation was opened in 1805, but unfortunately it didn't prove to be a great success. Barges could carry up to 50 tons pulled by one horse, or gangs of men called 'Halers', the keels they towed on the Foss were up to 55ft. long, 14ft. wide, and 5ft deep. The craft was crewed by one man and a boy. Halers were preferred to horses because they could cross the river easily when the towpath switched to the other side, it would be difficult to get the horse to the other side if the river was deep, or the banks were steep. Landings were constructed at various points along the Foss to load and unload cargoes of timber, coal, hay, gravel etc. The arrival of the York to Beverley railway line terminated the Foss navigation venture, and the last barge to use the section from Strensall to terminus was in 1852.

Church Lane Bridge

This bridge, built in 1860 was arched to allow the passage of barges down the River Foss. The parapets were added later. The change in the appearance of the brickwork is clearly visible.

West Huntington Hall

The original hall was built for Sir Arthur Ingram in 1629, and was rebuilt for Captain Sir Thomas Dowker around 1800. Access to the hall was either down Church Lane, or across the old bridge at the bottom of Mill Hill. Later, a new swing bridge was built when the River Foss became navigational *(See page 34)*. The Hall has had both residential and business use. During the Second World War, the coach house behind the Hall *(see photo below)* was in use as the H.Q. for the Home Guard. It has since been transformed into a very impressive house by Mr and Mrs D Calam. Miss Ethel Newton, born in 1878, the well known local painter, lived there with her parents between 1914 and 1925.

West Huntington Hall Residents

1629	Sir Arthur Ingram	1914	Thomas Newton
1825	Captain Sir Thomas Dowker	1922	Mr C Wilkinson
1872	Captain William Driffield	1925	James Richardson
1886	Mrs Metcalf	1948	Army Kinema Cooperation
1897	Mrs Bindloss	1960	Peter Gray – Dental Surgeon
1901	E H Bindloss	1965	John Dosser
1909	Dowager Lady Austin	2003	Julian and Ruth Gladwin

Photo: Mr and Mrs D Calam

Huntington Church

The church is dedicated to All Saints, and is situated on the west bank of the River Foss. It is a small church built of brick and stone with a chancel, nave, north aisle, south porch and a western tower with a spire containing six bells. The bells were donated by the Mills family. The head of the family wanted to be buried in Huntington churchyard, and on his death his wishes were honoured. In appreciation, one bell was donated by each member of his family. The church was restored in 1874, when the church doorway was removed and relocated further back. When the wooden steeple was taken down, two and a half stones of honey was found.

Photo: Tony Roberts

The Driffield family from West Huntington Hall worshipped there. The children of the family were beset with tragedy, most of whom died very young. One of their sons, a naval officer, drowned whilst rescuing an Irish M.P. His parents presented the church with an organ in his memory. An interesting feature is the rings in the wall near the door, where the worshippers tethered their horses *(see page 70)*. In 1877, a lych-gate was donated by public subscription. For years it formed a backdrop to many wedding photographs. The vicar during the late 1970s, arranged for it to be removed and taken to Easingwold church, against the wishes of the Parish Council and many local village residents. The church formed a scout troop in 1913, and they received their colours in 1931. A Girl Guides group was formed in 1929.

The vicarage *(left)* was built in 1902. The current vicar lived here until it was decided to put it up for sale.

Huntington Methodist Church

The Life Boys

Photo: Geoff Brayshaw

The Life Boys were the junior section of the Boys Brigade and were members of the Methodist Church, Nancy Leeming is on the left, next to her is Eva Magson.

The present chapel next to the Memorial Hall was built in 1900 on land donated by John Hoyle.

The spire was struck by lightening in 1925, and as a result of the damage, leakage occurred between the spire and the chapel. In 1935, the spire was removed. The iron railings shown in the picture were taken away during 1941 to assist the war effort.

A highlight for children in the 1920s was the Easter picnic. Everyone would meet at the village pond, (where the doctor's surgery is now, at the junction of North Moor Road and North Lane), then walk up North Lane to Crompton Woods. Miss Magson led the Easter Monday mystery tour for pupils on bicycles, which went further away to places such as Kirkham Abbey. Another popular event was the Annual Anniversary when all children were found a place, with a song or poem ready and new summer clothes. White straw hats for the girls could be bought for sixpence halfpenny at Boyes stores, and decorated at home. The most popular event was the annual trip to the coast. Local farmers and tradesmen took school children to Strensall station in their carts. About sixty children and twelve teachers travelled on the train to Scarborough. After a day at the seaside they would have tea at Westborough or Queen Street Chapel schoolrooms hired for under £1.

Photo: Tony Roberts

St. Andrew's Church

The building of the New Earswick village brought about the need for an extra church in the area. St. Andrew's was built in 1913 under the instruction of Rev. Edwin Storre Fox. The architect was Edwin Crumbie of Huntington. The church was extended in 1938 to accommodate the increasing congregation.

Other Items of Interest

THE FONT. The bowl of the Font is very much older than St. Andrew's church and is reported to have stood in an earlier church at Huntington. The pedestal and base are of a more recent period.

OAK FURNITURE. The Lectern, Clergy Stalls, Litany Desk and Communion Rails were made by Messrs. Thompson of Kilburn and each piece bears their famous mouse mark.

THE PROCESSIONAL CROSS. The wood of this Cross was cut from a tree at Fountains Abbey and was made by the late Mr. Herbert Wheeler of New Earswick, at one time a Churchwarden at St. Andrew's.

THE STONE CUBE. Forming the 'heel stone' for the Mothers' Union Banner, the cube was made for St. Andrew's Church by a Czech refugee from the 1939-45 War.

Laying the extension foundation stone on 18 June 1938

St. Andrew's Church Lads & Girls Brigade

Photo: Martin Stubbs

The Brigade Company at St. Andrew's was started in 1983. The band was formed in 1987 with the acquisition of 3 trumpets shortly followed by 3 side drums and a bass drum. Initially, the trumpeters were instructed by a member of the Salvation Army. Over the years they have been successful in progressing through the Novice and Contest classes, and into the Championship section culminating in 2007 by winning the competition outright, and becoming Supreme Champions.

1st Huntington Scout Band

Larry Gray formed the scout band in 1964. He was an adult leader who had been with the group since he was eleven. They relied on help from people who had experience of drum and bugle bands, but they did not stay long with the band because of other commitments. I became involved when during a chance meeting with Larry, whom had I known from my time in the scouts. I mentioned I had been in the Army cadet and Territorial Army bands as a Drummer/bugler, and I asked if I could attend a band practice. He agreed, and I remained a part of the group for six years. Larry's good leadership and enthusiasm coupled with my instruction, which I enjoyed, meant we had a really good band. It still exists to this day.

Local Beat Groups and Bands

The Clubmen

Graham Cambridge and Anton Betteridge, two of my friends from the North Moor Estate bought guitars in 1960, and started to learn Shadows instrumental music. I was at the time a drummer in the Territorial Army, and they invited me to join them at practice sessions. At first I was reluctant, but after a few sessions, began to take more interest. We eventually got a rhythm guitarist, David Bicknall, who like myself, came from New Earswick. We practiced at Hopwood's slaughterhouse (Anton worked there) and after a few months we were ready to play local gigs. The first bookings at the Memorial hall and the Folk Hall New Earswick, gave us confidence and improved our musical standard. We then moved into venues in York and other towns.

Left to right James Beck, Dave Bicknell – Rhythm, Graham Cambridge – Bass, Colin Carr – Drums and Anton Betteridge – Lead Guitar & Vocals.

The photo *(left)* was taken of us in the Royal Box at the Theatre Royal, York, when we played incidental music for the play 'Semi Detached' in 1963. James Beck was the leading man and later became famous starring in 'Dad's Army' as Private Walker (the spiv).

The Vampires

Another local group in the 1960s was the Vampires, which was formed by Ray Hill. The other two guitarists were Dave Earnshaw and Mick Barker, They didn't have a permanent drummer. They also played at local dances.

Left to right Dave Earnshaw – Lead Guitar, A. N. Other – Drums, Ray Hill – Bass and Mick Barker – Rhythm Guitar.

The Stars and Stripes

The band was formed by Mike Brown from Huntington in the mid 1970s. The original members were pupils of Huntington Secondary Modern School, and as the name suggests, they played the Glen Miller Big Band sound, appearing at not only local venues, but at many places beyond the city of York. I attended some of their concerts a few times, and felt they had achieved an extremely good standard, especially as the average age would have been about fifteen years of age.

Photo: Pat Johnson

The Mike Vevers Band

Photo: Mike Vevers

The band, formed in 1970, performing as resident musicians at the Huntington Working Men's Club, has had several different members since and is approaching forty years performing at the club. This line up shows, on drums Mike Vevers, bass Dick Hattie, sax Ted Gee and Duncan Grant on piano. The band still plays for dances every Friday night at the club.

Local Pubs

The White Horse

The White Horse was situated in Main Street, on the right hand corner of Pear Tree Close. In the Huntington church notes, a reference is made to vestry meetings held in the House of Thomas Cass, (The White Horse) in 1838. The landlord in 1867 was Charlie Carr. I visited the pub in 1960, but it wasn't as popular as the Blacksmith Arms (Blackies), and it eventually closed and was demolished around 1970. The last landlord was Mr. Creaser. The only evidence of the pubs existence is a nearby road called White Horse Close.

The Hare and Hounds

This pub dates from before 1800, the landlord in 1823 was Wm. Dixon. John Prentice kept the house in 1867. It was later converted into farmhouse, but it is not known when. (*See Bullock's Farm page 16*)

The Blacksmith's Arms

Photo: Hugh Murray

Originally called the Hammer and Pincers, the 'Blackies', took its name from the blacksmith's shop which was next to the pub, until it moved over the road to the Walnuts in 1900.

Below is a list of landlords from 1823.

1823   John Varley, a victualler and blacksmith.
1840   Robert Varley, probably his son, took over, he was also a blacksmith.
1867   Wm. Dixon.
1876   John Rispin.
1898   George Slater.
1909   Wm. Burke.
1930s   Willy Hirst.

Percy (Smudger) Smith, and his wife Queenie became landlord and landlady in 1944. Queenie had worked there as a barmaid during the war, for Willy Hirst, and when Percy returned after war service in the Green Howards, he became the landlord. I visited the 'Blackies' many times during the 60s and 70s, and was often served by Percy. He had been a Sergeant Major in the army so trouble was very rare.

Royal Visit

Queen Elizabeth, the Queen Mother waves to the regulars as she passes in 1950, probably on her way to the Queen Elizabeth barracks at Strensall.

The Slip Inn

The Slip Inn 1930

Photo: Hugh Murray

The Slip Inn was situated on the Malton Road, half a mile past the Hopgrove Inn, in the direction of York. It comprised two small rooms and had a very good darts team. The dartboard had a gas mantle lamp above which dried the double top. This resulted in the darts falling out, so players who knew about this always went for double 19 instead. There was also another gas lamp above the throwing line (the oche). Tall players had to stand to one side or get burnt. The gas mantle lamps and outside toilets were still there when the pub was demolished in 1968. All that remains of the Slip Inn is a kerb stone recess at the side of Malton Road. A family called Granger lived here for many years.

The Flag and Whistle

The Flag and Whistle is built on the former site of the Earswick railway Station circa: 1982. It is a pleasant pub providing meals and entertainment.

Huntington Working Men's Club

The club came about when a group of people gathered in a field at Manor farm in 1924, to discuss the possibility of the village having its own club. They acquired an old brick cowshed on the site of the present club, set about cleaning it up, and doing alterations to make it habitable. There was a house called Ivy Cottage near the cowshed, which was Tutil's farmhouse, and was later owned by the club. The modified cowshed was later extended and joined up to the cottage. This was used by the ARP and AFS during the war. It was demolished in the 1950s. There was an outdoor toilet for the ladies at the front. Mrs. Rene Magson recalls the path to it having a trellis fence covered in sweet smelling roses, which were lovely in the summertime. All sections of the club, which included football, cricket and fishing, held annual social evenings. There was a horticultural show every September, and club trips. Rabbit pie suppers were a popular feature for many years. One occasion being the anniversary of the club foundation, and during the war years, for the Home Guard. These meals were served in the cowshed. The pies were made in the cottage and passed through a window.

Committee members receive ten year service awards

Photo: Huntington WMC

The large concert room was built in 1966. The top of the bill for the opening night was Max Wall. Other artists that have appeared during the 1960s included Albert Modley, Acker Bilk, Lance Percival, David Whitfield, Carl Denver, Charlie Williams, Lynn Perry, Liz Dawn and Freddy and the Dreamers. All of whom either were, or became popular television performers.

In the 1950s, a local lady called Nellie Magson played the piano, and accompanied many performers. The first resident band consisted of Mr. Plues who played the Hawaiian guitar, and his son David who played guitar. The band also had a drummer and a bass guitarist. They produced a very unique sound. In 1968, they were followed by the Mike Vevers Band who are still there in 2008. I remember a great night in the 1990s, when they had the well known big band drummer, Eric Delaney. He was supported by a witty comedian, and at the time an unknown singer called, Jane McDonald. It was packed out and every one enjoyed the evening.

Huntington WMC cricket team during the 1960s

Photo: Len Watson

The club is still thriving, although people's social habits change, and like all the other clubs, they are not as full as they used to be, unless it's a special occasion. The snooker room is very popular. There are very active sections for fishing, golf etc. Annual trips are organised, and each Christmas there is a pantomime for the children.

Ladies Walking Match
Participants *(above)* pose for a photograph in 2005
Photo: Jack Smith

Huntington Sports Club

The club was built in the early 1980s, with voluntary help given by its members. It has two football teams, two cricket teams, petanque and a golf society. Indoor recreation includes Pool, darts and dominoes. Occasional social functions are also catered for, and the club also hosts the local branch of the Shadows Guitar Club once a month.

Swallow Cottage

Mr. and Mrs. W. Wregglesworth who currently own Swallow Cottage on North Lane, gave me a small extract from their house deeds and is shown below.

1/8/1922 The Right Honourable Lady Alwyne Compton Vyner of Newby Hall, sold a piece of land to Walter Magson in the first part. Most Hon. Frederick Oliver Marquess of Ripon.

William Arthur Tilney of Sutton Binnington in Nottingham, of second and Walter Magson of the Post Office Huntington, purchaser for £27 : 10s, triangular piece of land east side of Back Lane and north side of North Lane, no. 437 ordnance map.

26/2/1924 W.M. Magson sold (£620) to Arthur William Longbottom of the Hut, Chestnut Avenue, Heworth (Bank clerk), land and recently erected bungalow Brumber Cottage. The name was later changed to Swallow Cottage.

Huntington Fish Shop

Benny Pindar sold fish and chips from a wooden shop which was where the Huntington Service Station is currently located. In 1951 he had a house built with an adjoining shop, at the junction of North Moor Road and Keswick Way. His successor was Jack Booth. Bill Newbould from Rawdon took over in 1963, and the 'chippie' is currently owned by his son Ken.

Huntington Service Station

Local lad, Les Hunter (left) was an apprentice at Watsons Garage in the 1960s.

The garage was built for Maurice Watson in 1952 by local builders, Bradley and Wainhouse, the roof was added by Maurice, his son-in-law and other volunteers. When completed, he repaired cars and sold Esso petrol. He also owned two coaches which were parked alongside the garage. A local family called Shann has owned the garage for many years.

The Back Lane

Since the village existed, the main road travelled through the old village. After the Second World War, the prefabs were built, and with the North Moor Estate being constructed in 1947, the narrow track known as Back Lane was widened, which diverted heavy traffic away from Main Street. Buildings in the old Back Lane were few before 1946, until the prefabs arrived. A lone cottage stood on Mr. Imeson's land at the end of what is now Pear Tree Close. There were no other buildings until the White House (see page 16), opposite the village pond. During the 1950s, small businesses started to appear. Benny Pindar sold fish and chips from a wooden hut. There was also garage, a paper shop and Watson's coaches. Beyond the current library in Garth Road, was an old country lane, called Mucky Trotters Lane *(see page 68)*. In the 1920/30s, a large van with catering equipment would arrive and park on the corner of North Lane, opposite the village pond (where the doctor's surgery is now), and for two weeks each year, girls from the Board School would be taught cooking skills. During WWII two wooden huts were built on the grass verge not far from the vicarage to house two trailer pumps and equipment belonging to the local Auxiliary Fire Service *(see page 27)*.

John Bullock driving his horse and cart along Back Lane on his way to his fields near Mucky Trotter's Lane in 1941.

Photo: Charles Bowerman

An elderly man makes his way through the snow *(right)* along Back Lane in 1940.

Photo: Mrs Freda Goodrick

This row of cottages, Garth End, was built by Flaxton Rural District Council in 1938. They were specifically built for families who were living in sub-standard houses, or were overcrowded.

The Prefabs

At the end of the Second World War, many houses were needed for the men returning from war service, and for those that had lost their homes through enemy action. It would take years to re-establish the building trade, which had declined because so many tradesmen had been away at war. To kick-start the process, Flaxton Rural District Council, who had been allocated 50 Tarran pre-fabricated (hence the name Prefab) buildings imported from the USA. 21 were installed in Huntington by Freddy Shepherd on North Moor Road, in front of the proposed new North Moor Estate. These were built in 1946, leaving a gap for the access road to the new estate, which was built in 1947. Although the prefabs were built to provide temporary accommodation, the people who lived in them were very satisfied, and didn't want to move. This temporary period was to last 50 years until they were finally demolished around 1995, and were replaced with bungalows. A sample was saved, and is to be seen at the Eden Camp museum near Malton.

Mrs. Freda Goodrick

Enid and Freda Lawson at the Fourth Milestone Farm 1939

Freda moved to the Fourth Milestone Farm from Skipton in 1936. She attended Huntington School, and recalls a new bridge being built over the railway line on the Malton Road, and evacuees from Hull arriving and being billeted in the Memorial Hall. She also remembers Maurice Watson (senior) had a threshing machine, and went round the farms where local farmers helped to man the stacks, and conveyers carried the corn bags to the granary. "My sister and I went to Sunday School. The teachers were, Misses Magson, Bakes and Nelson. The highlights of the year were the anniversaries and the annual trip to the coast, by train from Strensall station. In 1940, we moved to Bakewell. In the early 1950s, I met my future husband Ted Goodrick, and married in 1952. We eventually moved into the cottage on North Moor Road, belonging to Mr. Imeson. I called it 'Gwen Mawr'. Ted had his own joinery business and worked from a shed on Imeson's land. In 1962, Ted built his own house not far from the old cottage. It was a revolutionary style of building and was the first of its kind in the area."

The cottage before demolition in 2004

'Gwen Mawr'

Ted Goodrick and friend

Freda outside Ted's workshop

The Goodrick family had a friend called Eric Bissitt, who was very popular with the locals. He organised trips with 'SAGA' for local 'senior citizens'. He died on 28 May, 1972. The photo below shows villagers and parish councillors gathering round the seat donated in his memory.

J. E. GOODRICK

JOINER, UNDERTAKER
AND PAINTER

NORTH MOOR ROAD
HUNTINGTON

Tel. 68682

Photo: Mrs Freda Goodrick

Local Farms

For many years, Huntington had an average of 25 farms, but in the 1950s/60s because of mechanisation, and food being imported from abroad, they were on the decline.

Breck's Lodge

Formerly Pearson's dairy, it is now Cottrell's, who sell new and used lawnmowers. They also supply spare parts, servicing and repairs, including sharpening garden shears.

Huntington Grange

Formerly a dairy farm owned by the well known Bowling family. It is now a cattery.

Local Farms

Hopwood's Garden Farm

Formerly Edwin Hopwood's, it now stands derelict. Of interest is the old earth closet *(above right)* in the farmyard, and is typical of farms and houses built before 1900.

The Tithe Barn

Manor Farm is a very old building on the corner of Huntington Road and New Lane, which has a Tithe barn. Tithe means one tenth, and represents the amount of tax that would be paid on the buildings many years ago. It was originally Ward's Farm, but is now managed by Bob Stokel.

The Poplars Farm

The Poplars farm belonged to Barton's of York. It was farmed for years by the Yates family and passed from father to son. Mr. Alf Yates used to take part in the Huntington carnivals in the 1920s/30s by decorating one of his horse drawn carts and competing against other farmers. After the long parade the carts ended up at West Huntington Hall. Alf always came first or second, and later, his biggest rival was his son, Walter, who also did well in the competition. I have old press cuttings of these events. An aerial view of the farm is shown above. Huntington Secondary Modern School was built on this site around 1970, and on completion the farm was demolished.

Mrs. Kathleen Watson (formerly Kathleen Yates) lived on this farm as a young girl, and has many fond and happy memories of her life there.

Above is one of the many Charles Bowerman's photographs of Walter Yates ploughing with horses. I have been told, his furrows were always as straight as a die.

Photo: Cath Watson

Huntington and Earswick Carnival

Photo: Cath Watson

Walter Yates pictured above, with his decorated cart, or 'Rulley' as they were known, outside his father's house in New Lane which is still there.

The Carnival was a popular annual event held on August Bank Holiday Mondays. It was held in the grounds of West Huntington Hall. In the 1920s, money was raised for local buildings such as Huntington Memorial Hall, or one of the churches. A large parade of decorated carts and people in fancy dress travelled on a route via Earswick, Huntington, Yearsley Bridge, Haley's Terrace, and New Earswick. One year, the parade was lead by the L.N.E.R. Comic Band, and was 300yds long. An extra field adjoining the hall was loaned by Major Unett, to accommodate the large number of carts and people taking part. There were competitions for the best decorated carts, a horticultural show and children's sports. There was dancing round the Maypole, folk dancing and a display of Highland dancing by the 2bn. Royal Scots Fusiliers. Adult sports which were held in the evening, were followed by entertainment in the Memorial Hall. On one occasion the evening entertainment was; Mrs. Richardson-elocutionist, Miss. Masser-soprano soloist, Mr. Chapman-tenor vocalist, Mr. Asquith-Siffleur, Mr. Holmes-humorist. The evening culminated with a grand dance. For at least 8 years the money raised went to the Memorial Hall. On one occasion it went to the church tower restoration fund (£92), the following year it was hoped that a debt of £100 owed would be cleared.

York and North Midland Railway Company

On the 4 October 1847, the York to Market Weighton and Beverley railway line was completed, which passed through Huntington from the Earswick Station, over New Lane, North Lane and across the Malton Road. The original station was next to the crossing gates on New Lane, and this building still remains, although it has been extensively modernised. The current owner, who bought it in 1968,

tells me there was still a platform there then, but it has since been removed, and also what appeared to be a hatch which was probably the ticket office. Later, the Earswick Station was built, with sidings in the station yard, which often had full coal trucks there waiting to be unloaded by coal merchants. Hall's leatherworks, which was built next to the station in 1910, also had their own private siding.

One of the sidings (*pictured left*) was behind the signal box. This was located on the site of the old Eborcraft factory on Huntington Road. The Haxby Road crossing can be seen in the background.

Passing the raised signal box where Eborcaft was, opposite the station, the track continued eastwards, and crossed the road at New Lane where the current entrance to Portakabin is. On the way to the North Lane crossing an avenue of trees currently marks the route which the track took. The crossing keeper's house is still there. It has been a guest house, but is now a private residence, which is largely hidden from view, but the traditional railway style chimneys remain. The line fell victim to the Beeching cuts, and the last train ran in 1965. I remember very well the railway in the 1950s, local families would board the train at Earswick station, and go to Stamford Bridge for a day out especially during the summer. The trains went over a bridge above the River Foss, and I remember as a boy standing under the bridge as a train went over, it was very noisy and you could see the underside of the train through the girders of the bridge. A pub was built on the site of the station in the early 1980s, and is called appropriately, the Flag and Whistle, (see page 44).

Railway bridge over the River Foss which is now the Link Road.

It is believed by some that this house, which is on New lane opposite the entrance to Portakabin, was the original Huntington station before the Earswick station was in use.

Early station masters were: George Parker c:1867, John Henry Lamb c:1893 and Charles Brown c:1901.

These two cottages were for the crossing gatekeepers, and situated close to the junction of North Lane and Malton Road. The first crossing was about fifty yards from the top of North Lane, and the second, on Malton Road. (A64) close to Fourth Milestone Farm. A railway bridge was built over the track on the A64 in 1936. When the York to Beverley line was closed, the cottages were sold off. A young married couple bought one. The husband had been in the Royal Canadian Air force during the war, and so they called their home 'Maple Cottage' as a reminder of home, and remains so to this day. The railway bridge was demolished in the early the 1980s.

Yorkshire Clubs Brewery

The Loco Brewery at Pocklington, which was so named because of the town's connection with the railway, moved to Huntington in 1934, into a newly built brewery on New Lane. At the height of production it had a workforce of around fifty, and supplied beer to Huntington WMC and other clubs in the area. Houses were built in 1936 for some of the brewery workers and were called Brewery Cottages. They remain so to this day, as do the wrought iron railings which fronted the brewery. There was a character from New Earswick called Jack Pavis, who had land behind the cottages where he had a small holding and he kept pigs. He also had a horse and cart. In those days such people were called 'carters'. He used to bring hops and malt from the Earswick station to the brewery on his cart. On the way back he would park his horse and cart outside the club, and go in for a drink. On occasions, the horse must have become impatient, and made its own way back to the brewery while Jack was enjoying his drink.

Photo: Mike Willis

The brewery which closed in 1968 was demolished in 1973. Brewing equipment was donated to the Beamish museum with the intention of recreating a brewery. Tragically, one of the men dismantling some of the equipment was crushed by a heavy section of metal and killed.

Brewery Drays in the 1940s *(pictured left)*. Note the masks on the headlights and the white edges on the mudguards, so they could be seen during the wartime blackout.

Brewery Cottages built 1936

Photo:Mike Willis

This large house at the junction of Jockey Lane and New Lane which is now as an agency for the Halifax Bank and other financial services, was originally the house of the head brewer, but later was to become the home of brewery secretary Mr. A. Willis and his family.

Pictured above are the original wrought iron railings that fronted the brewery site

The Police House

This house, which is opposite the Memorial Hall on Strensall Road, also was the police station, purpose built for the village policeman, complete with an underground prison cell. In the 1950s and 1960s P.C. Jackson resided there with his two sons Barry and Grant. Barry played for York City Football Club for many years.

East Huntington Hall

The photo shows Mrs. Thelma Wadsworth playing miniature golf in the hall grounds

The Hall was almost opposite the Memorial Hall until it was demolished around 1970. In the 1920s, an ex army officer, Captain Henry Unett, J.P. for the East Riding of Yorkshire, was resident. Later in the 1950s, a lady called Mrs. Drew lived there. She was a very enthusiastic member of Huntington church, and often had fund raising events in the hall grounds for the church. She was known for always being very well dressed, wore very large Hats and spoke very 'upper class'.

A visit to Huntington in 1937 by the Yorkshire Herald

A reporter accompanied by a talented sketcher paid a visit to Huntington to find out more about the locals and sketch caricatures of the interviewees. The sketches are recreated below. A transcript of interviews with well known members of the community is also printed below, in the order they were carried out.

Willy Hirst

The first port of call was the Blacksmiths Arms to meet the landlord, Willy Hirst, "Fra Pudsey". First, they looked at the old pump at the rear of the pub dated 1823, and found the water 'delicious'. Willy told us there were folk in the village who remember the thatched cottages, he said "when you take the thatched cottages away, You take the country itself away".

He remarked about town folk migrating to council estates, and the country folk don't like it. We are doing away with the slums and sending the people to the estates in the suburbs.

Mr R J Wolstenholme

Mr. Wolstenholme, a retired schoolmaster, and has been treasurer of the parish church for 25 years. He took up his post as schoolteacher in 1899, and was there for 33 years. He supported the need for a road from Huntington to Haxby, he spoke to a lady the other day who had not been to Haxby for 30 years. He opposed the new drainage scheme, he thinks it is too expensive and there are cheaper ways of doing It.

Mrs Magson

The next visit was to see the village postmistress, Mrs. Magson, she has lived in Huntington since she was a month old, and has seen many changes. Her daughters live with her and they helped us to persuade her to have her caricatures in the paper.

Mr John Rank

John Rank is the village verger and sexton for Huntington church, he told me the church dates from around 1300 and has belonged to the Dean and Chapter of York Minster since the 15th century. There are six peals of bells and the last time they were rung was when John and his wife celebrated their golden wedding anniversary, in honour of them both, the York Minster bell ringers rang the merry peal.

Middleton Hunt

Photo: Eric Weightman

The hunt was based at Birdsall near Malton, and were invited to hunt by pub landlords or farmers. Local venues were, Huntington, Flaxton, Sand Hutton, Farlington, and Stockton on Forest. They usually took place on Wednesdays. Sometimes they would hunt in the low country, Sheriff Hutton, which was very flat, and on other occasions on the hills of the Yorkshire Wolds. In the event of a meet at a pub, the landlord would provide a Stirrup Cup, which would contain an unknown quantity of drink, with ginger or fruit cake. Lord Halifax rode with this hunt from 1945 to 1953. Another well known celebrity who rode with the hounds was local horseman, Colonel Henry Wellington Tutill Palmer. Col. Palmer, being local, very actively supported many events..The Hunt ball was held in Huntington Memorial Hall and was organised by Mr. L. Cottrell, of Brecks farm. Mrs. Josie Knowels, who rode with the hunt very often, also helped to prepare the food during the day, and decorate the stage with two stuffed foxes and other hunt related décor.

The Landau

Photo: Terry Berry

Mr. Ray Smith, who lives in Huntington, owns a landau (a carriage pulled by a horse). In addition to taking tourists round the centre of York, he provides transport for the bride and groom at weddings. He is shown (*above and left*) at the Knavesmire, and at Huntington church.

Eva Coates

Eva

Photo: J. C. Lacy

1 March 1907, 13 year old Eva Coates wrote to her elder sister Nellie, a pupil teacher in Hull about the latest news in Huntington. 'The old thatched cottage has tumbled at last. It was 12 noon when it happened. Poor Mrs. Plowman and her two children had to get through the window to get out, the children are with Mrs. Ward, and Mrs. Plowman is at Mr. Fox's.' John Lacy, a former Methodist minister, who is Eva's great nephew, has a collection of Eva's letters and photos of Huntington in the early 1900's. She details village gossip, which gives an insight into life in the village back then. One letter dated September 1906, describes a road accident involving a horse and cart. A little girl was going home and George Magson gave her a lift. When she got out of the cart, the horse moved forward and the cartwheel rolled over her foot. She was taken to hospital, and next day had two toes removed, and slightly later two more. Sadly, two weeks later she died of Lockjaw (the old name for Tetanus). She writes of a fat cattle show coming to the village, and the exploits of a runaway calf. Eva Coates died of consumption on Aug 3, 1907. Fortunately, she lives on in John Lacy's collection of letters and photographs.

Eva's house, which is situated halfway down the Old Village (Main Street).

Huntington Dairies and Milk Distributors

There have been several dairy farms and milk distributors over the years. Miss Hare delivered milk locally for many years after continuing her father's business. The Bowling family had a dairy farm at Huntington Grange *(see page 53)*. During the 1950s/60s, the Green family distributed milk from their home on Huntington Road opposite Mill Lodge (formally the Bungalow Hospital) Arbor Close.

Below are three milk distributors which were established in the early 1900s.

Miss Bertha Broadley

Bertha attended the Huntington Board school, and was a very bright scholar. She passed a scholarship exam and went to Queen Anne's Grammar School. Her aunty took her to Bridlington for a few days as a reward. At 14 she was taken ill with a weak heart, which confined her to bed for a year, and thus her education came to an end. She recalls, "by the time I had recovered properly it was nearly wartime and I joined my father's milk round business. It wasn't like it is now though and I delivered milk twice a day on my bike. I would cycle all over with my can of milk and a measuring cup fastened to the handlebars. Many of our customers were in New Earswick, but if they moved house they still wanted milk from us, so I used to cycle all the way to Dringhouses sometimes. It was quite hard work and I used to dread getting stuck in the tram lines."

When I lived in New Earswick as a boy, I remember Miss Broadley, who delivered our milk. Occasionally I helped her on a Saturday morning. I would climb into the back of the van, which was a Jowett.

Tutil's Dairy

Mr. Charlie Tutil ran a dairy farm from Ivy Cottage, which was where the Working Men's Club is now. he is seen *(left)* with his milk float walking past Mille Crux Terrace towards Strensall Road.

Pearson's Dairy

Pearson's Dairy was in New Lane at Brecks Lodge, now Cottrell's, (see page 53) and was there for many years until the 1950s.

The Pearson Family circa: 1930 *(right)*.

Items of Local Historical Interest

The Water Pump

The landlord of the Blacksmith's Arms, Percy Algernon (Smudger) Smith draws water from the pump which until recently was behind the pub. It was dated 1823. Where did it go?

The Gate to the Old Hall

During a visit to West Huntington Hall, the owners, Julian and Ruth Gladwin showed me this wrought iron gate which had originally been at the hall's main entrance.

Coffin Walk

This walk started at Hopgrove Lane, close to the pub of the same name on Malton Road (A1036), and went across the fields in the direction of Huntington North, then crossing the railway lines it followed the beck to North Lane. It is said that this was the most direct route for the pall bearers carrying a coffin from the Hopgrove area to Huntington church. The route continued across what is now North Moor Road, to the snicket which terminated next to Prospect House.

Until the 1960s, there was a wooden stile at the end of this snicket, which at one time had a platform 'rest' for the coffin built in. After a short rest, the bearers would cross the village Main Street to Church Lane directly opposite, for the last leg of the journey. There was also a 'corpse path' which started at the Wigginton pond, followed the route of the Westfield beck towards New Earswick, across what is now the front of Joseph Rowntree's school and approached Huntington church from the North.

Post Office Clock

Huntington church records show that in 1882, the public subscribed to provide a clock which was placed on the wall of the then village Post Office at a cost of £8: 10s. The occupants had the task of winding it up once a week. When Dr. and Mrs. N.C. Porter lived there in the 1950s, the villagers, the postman and the policeman used to stand and check their watches, "but we got used to it" said Mr. And Mrs. Porter.

Mucky Trotter's Lane

This country lane starts soon after passing Garth End cottages and carries on to open fields. Pigs used to be kept in this area, which could explain the origin of the name. Until the 1960s, someone lived in an old railway carriage in this vicinity.

Sleeper Path

This link between New Earswick and Huntington Road was originally made of old wooden railway sleepers. I remember seeing them in the 1950s and they were in a state of decay. At one end of the path was St. Andrew's church, and at the other end, this side of the river, outside the New Earswick village boundary, was Harry Bradley's fish shop. At that time, the Joseph Rowntree Village Trust wouldn't allow a fish and chip shop in the village of New Earswick. Although it was a path, I remember small vehicles and carts using it. Later, a proper road was built, but posts were erected at each end to deter motorists from using it. Since the Link Road was built on the former railway line, it is only used by pedestrians.

The Pinfold

A pinfold was opposite the Board School on Main Street, and would have been a small brick surround with a gate. The purpose of the pinfold was to keep stray cattle and other animals in until the farmer came to collect them. In 1843, the vestry passed a bylaw which stated that any stray animals would be impounded in the pinfold, and a fine would have to be paid for their release. The fines levied included 1s : 6p (8 new pence) for· a donkey. The Huntington pinfold has long gone, but a sample still exists in the village of Hunmanby. *(See below).*

The Poor houses

As the name suggests these cottages were for poor people who would have received financial help from the parish. They were probably built in the 1700s, and sadly demolished about 1995. There was a well over the road, and a local man remembers it being used by the people living in the cottages. In the 1960s, I entered one of these cottages, and I remember how low the height of the doors were. They became a centre for elderly people during the 1970s, called 40/70s Club.

Huntington Church Wall Tether Rings

The rings *(as illustrated above)* were used by worshippers to tether their horses.

The Butter Cross

There are four round recesses in the top of the Butter Cross surrounding what is left of the stem. Originally it would have been quite tall so the cross at the top of the stem would be seen by wandering lepers and homeless people. There are several Butter Crosses in the York area.

Local Vintage Vehicles

Motor Carrier Service

This old bus dating from the 1920s, provided a service between Strensall and York, there were no official bus stops then, and passengers holding there hand out would be picked up any where along the route.

Watsons Coaches

Maurice Watson standing proudly beside his well polished Ford Thames coach, circa: 1960.

Local Vintage Vehicles

There are several vintage vehicle owners in Huntington. A selection is shown below.

The car pictured *(left)* is a 1952 Jowett Jupiter. Only 1000 were manufactured. This one is owned by Mr. Peter Stokel.

The Ford Jeep *(right)* built in 1945, was owned by Colin Swales who has since sold it and bought an air portable Land Rover.

An early 1930s Jowett, made specially for a tailor with a high roof to hang suits without creasing them.

An ex army Austin 10 utility pickup is pictured *(right)*. They were commonly called 'Tillys' which was an abbreviation of 'utility'. These vehicles were used as general runabouts. The one featured was used on the island of Malta during WWII.

Another rare Jowett under restoration, nearing completion and looking good.

Tony Agar's Mosquito

The fuselage is rolled out of Tony's drive, on its way to the Yorkshire Air Museum.

A former Huntington resident, Tony Agar, claimed fame for the village by starting building a full sized Mosquito aircraft in his garden. Tony first became interested in the Mosquito when attending an Air Training Corps camp he saw a model of one at an exhibition, when he returned home, he set about making his own. May years later, he visited a Mosquito crash site and brought some parts home. From then on, he had made up his mind to rebuild a complete Mosquito. After acquiring a cockpit and a fuselage the building started in his garage. At the same time, the Yorkshire Air Museum was founded and soon after, Tony was invited to take his rebuild there, this enabled him to put his fuselage under cover being a huge advantage. Many years later, the aircraft was 'rolled out' to be admired by countless people, a tribute to a man's dedication.

Steptoe Lives On!

A very rare sight nowadays but pleasing to see, a scrap man collecting surplus modern high tech metal household commodities with his horse and cart in Huntington 2011.

The Young Ones

Silver Moor Youth Club – Circa: 1958-65

Photo: Pete Freeman – boy seated front far right

Mr. Ernie Cambridge was always on the sports field organising sports and games on an evening. Attempts had been made to form a youth club without success, so Ernie and his wife Violet formed a committee which included, Arthur Winup, Mrs. Wade, Mrs. Tallot, Mrs. Betteridge and Harold Harrison. The youth club met at the Memorial Hall each week, where games and P. T. were organised. There was also a monthly dance, when members would bring the latest records in the charts. The highlight of the year was the annual sports day. A tent would be borrowed from the army at Strensall, and used as the 'officials tent'. Ernie's son, Graham and myself would go and collect it with an old pram. Football games would be played and also all kinds of races and athletics. A competition was held for the girls when a Carnival Queen would be chosen. In the evening a dance would be held, and sometimes a local beat group, The Clubmen, would play the current hits of the sixties.

Huntington Primary School

In 1966, an event was opened by Blue Peter presenter Christopher Trace (*see right*).

Photo: Kate Earp

The Foss Patrol

Myself and friends on an Army cadet 'jungle warfare exercise' cooling our feet on a hot Sunday afternoon. The location is the bend in the River Foss near the boundary of West Huntington Hall. I am behind the section leader who is at the front. Graham Cambridge is at the rear.

Post War Development in Huntington

Described by Mr. G. A. W. Heppell

Mr. Heppell left school in 1938 and started work as a junior clerk with the Flaxton Rural District Council in Bootham, York. He spent four of the war years in the army, and seven years away working for other rural district councils. He returned to Flaxton Rural District Council and retired in 1974 as Chief Environmental Health Officer and Housing Manager. Mr.Heppell has very kindly given his time, and the benefit of his knowledge to describe the building explosion of Huntington in the 1960s.

The vast expansion of Huntington to meet the increasing demands of York was on land designated by the North Riding County Council as the planning authority. There were several main developers.

R. J. Pulleyn and Sons

R. J. Pulleyn and Sons already owned Huntington Grange Farm on New Lane with land running southwards towards the River Foss at Huntington Road. The Highthorn estate consisted almost entirely of traditional small semi-detached houses, and was developed over a number of years. R. J. Pulleyn was a former Lord Mayor of York who had five or six sons; all were trained in some aspect of building work. I recall that Wilson ran the office, the City Garage in Blake Street and the Grand Cinema in Clarence Street, Fred was a joiner (I think) and Vic a mechanic who later opened up his own garages. The youngest, Jim, who was at school with me, did site work and eventually struck out on his own.

Jack Bradley and Phillip Wainhouse

Jack Bradley joined up with Phillip Wainhouse to form the Bradley Company. They first built two houses at the top end of Park Avenue, New Earswick, and then some traditional semis next to the vicarage at Huntington. They then got two architects, Tom Adams and Brian Cade (a local lad) to work for them, and they designed the bungalows on a module, and got them more highly organised when they built the Woodlands Way estate and then others further afield.

Sawdon and Simpson

Sawdon and Simpson was a brother and sister firm – Bill Sawdon and his sister Rachel; she was the organiser, he the site man. The firm was later run by Rachel's two sons David and Christopher. Brockfield Road was a small un-made road of nice detached houses before it became the access to their Brockfield Park Estate which ran through to New Lane.

Reg and Eric Todd

Broome Close on Strensall Road was built by Reg and his brother Eric, who were an old Huntington family.

Magson's Builders

Gormire Avenue, etc. was built by one of the local Magson builders.

Business in Huntington

Since the early 1900s, many businesses have been established in Huntington. The largest employers currently are Wm. Sessions printers, who opened a factory on Huntington Road in 1920, and Portakabin who came to New Lane in the early 1960s. Others were Eborcraft (furniture manufacturers) also Huntington Road, H.W. Gill and Sons (removal and haulage) and also the two long gone establishments featured below.

Henry Hall & Sons Ltd.

The photo *(left)* shows the tannery and currying works owned by Henry Hall. The company commenced business in York in 1780, then relocated to the pleasant site adjoining Earswick Station in 1910.

G W Hopwood & Sons

Hopwood's licensed slaughterhouse and knacker's yard was one of the few places in the country where the two businesses were run together. The premises were situated on the site currently occupied by The Range shopping centre. The business was very unpopular with local residents because of the terrible smell, and smoke that emitted from the large chimney. In the early 1960s, Malcolm Hopwood and his brother, who owned the firm, put a large notice board up at the end of Jockey Lane warning people who were considering buying a house in the area. Anton Betteridge, a local lad, worked in the dog meat shop at Hopwoods. When things were quiet in the shop, he used to practice on his guitar. He later formed a group in which I was the drummer called The Clubmen, (see page 40), and Malcolm let us practice in one of his buildings. He was very good to us, taking the band to gigs in his Landrover. He even took the band to see the Beatles at the Rialto in York, paying for all four of us.

G .W. Hopwood & Sons

CATTLE
DRESSING
CENTRE

★

TELEPHONE YORK 23755

NEW LANE, HUNTINGTON, YORK

Would You Believe It?

Lord Allen Spencer Churchill

Captain Sir Thomas Dowker, resident at West Huntington Hall, circa: 1820-1850, had a daughter called Rosamund, who was engaged to Lord Allen Spencer Churchill, (3rd son of the Duke of Marlborough) the great uncle of Lord Winston Churchill. The story goes that Lord Churchill, who was stationed at the York Cavalry Barracks, visited Rosamund, and was told that the bridge over the River Foss had been damaged, and he couldn't get across. He went to the thatched cottage near the Blacksmiths Arms, borrowed an old woman's clothes washing trough, and paddled himself across. Was it his quick thinking initiative that won the brides heart? They were married in July, 1846.

Jack Pavis

Jack was a popular character and could take a joke. Jack owned a horse and cart. On one occasion he had stopped off at the Working Men's Club for a drink. His horse had gone back to its stable area behind the Brewery Cottages, and waited at a barred gate. A practical joker, with some accomplices unhitched the horse and put the shafts of the cart through the bars of the gate and then harnessed the horse to the cart at the other side. I wonder what Jack made of this when he returned from the club?

The Dancing Pig

George Mills, who has lived in the village all his life, told me that when he worked on a local farm, one Saturday night, he and a friend took a young pig to the Memorial Hall where there was a dance in progress. He sneaked his hand inside the entrance and switched all the lights off. Then they both pushed the pig inside amongst all the dancers. It wouldn't have been only the pig that was squealing!

Foss Ice Cyclists

Paul Tutil tells me that when the river Foss froze during the severe winter of 1962, the ice was six inches thick. He and a few other lads cycled on the ice from Huntington to New Earswick. Local lad Les Harrison volunteered to lead the way.

The Thirsty Horse

Paul also tells me that his grandad, Charlie Tutil who had a dairy round, sometimes delivered milk in York. On the way back each day, the horse stopped at every pub and his grandad went in for a pint. When his son took over from him, the horse would stop as usual, and wouldn't move until he went into the pub and came out, not having had a drink.

In addition to liking a pint or two, his granddad also played dominos at the White Horse pub in the village. He was not a particularly good player, and often lost all his money. To pay his debts he would often have to resort to parting with one of his cows in payment.